# THE CHANGING CONSTITUTIONAL FRAMEWORK OF CHURCH-STATE RELATIONS IN EUROPE

MRIGANK GURUDATT

# Contents

# Preface

"Start writing, no matter what. The water does not flow until the faucet is turned on".

• Louis L'Amour

Hundreds of students and professors are contributing their work to Brillopedia, we are here to provide ample information about Law and Contemporary issues. Our aim is to provide a platform for today's generation to express their views and ideas on law and contemporary law.

# CHAPTER ONE

# ABSTRACT

The Research work focuses on a broad study of *Churchification of Europe* and the deep connection between the Constitutional State and the Papal diktats as they tussle for legitimacy in a sensitive space of Law, Human Rights & Authority that influence everyday life of People. The Research will analyse the Common thread binding the Church-State Relations through legislations over time and their impact on Contemporary society while drawing comparative study between the Church-State synergy in various European Countries as they step into a new era of Religious tolerance & Unity in Diversity by accompanying various faiths in the Social strata. The present state of nature of Christianity & God in Europe with many countries moving Post-WWII towards adopting an inclusive & secular system will also be covered in this analysis. Questions like *'What has been the nature of Church & State relationship historically?', 'Why the State moved away from the Supremacy of Pope?', 'Which European states supported & which opposed the pervasiveness of Christianity & God in Society?'* aresome of the questions that the Research aims to answer henceforth. A major gap has been found in the research work on legal status of religious groups which are neglected as European lawyers mainly focus on *Constitutional Textualism* rather than moulding their research to address the Socio-Legal reality. Another aspect will be studied where the Role of Churches shall be viewed from the perspective of European Integration & EU Politics which will pose some research challenges as Christian Churches are diverse in nature and are usually regarded as Non-State Actors like interest-groups, lobbyists, organisations of civil society, etc. The indirect connection between The European Convention for the Protection of Human Rights and Fundamental Freedoms (ECHR) and Church shall be examined with case precedents and its adoption into the National laws of major European states. The researcher also borrows from the practice adopted in United States and draws logical conclusion from the Indian perspective in this context with examples like Hijab Ban in France, Refugee Crisis in Europe, Religious Toleration in India etc. Till now the Changing Constitutional framework of Church-State Relations has been viewed from the lenses of *Conventional approach* where the Observation is categorised into: 1) State-Church Systems 2) Separation (Secular) Systems & 3) Hybrid (Cooperationist) Systems but now with the *New Approach* of scholars like Peter Huizing, major inferences can be drawn on the lacunae of the outdated classification which this work aims to Highlight.

# CHAPTER TWO

# INTRODUCTION

The relationship between State & Church has been key to the evolution of Europe into the Constitutional State we see today. This framework can be classified into: 1) **State-Church systems** which are characterized by close cooperation between State and a ReligiousCommunity like Christianity/ Church, Ex: England, Denmark, Greece, Finland, Bulgaria, Malta. 2) **Separation Systems** forbid the financial support & promotion of any one Religion as mandated in their constitution, Ex: France, The Netherlands, Ireland. 3) **Hybrid Systems** are those which lie between the above two and are characterized by a blend of the nature from the other two systems incl. commonality of tasks between the Church and State in the form of treaties, agreements & concordats, Ex: Austria, Italy, Spain, Belgium, Hungary, Portugal etc. This relationship has seen its ups & downs in countries like Germany & France during the Reformation & Revolution era but mostly it has seen wider acceptance among the Western European States. Initially the State and Church were linked by a common thread of Religious Uniformity which gradually changed as the State became dominant in Sanctioning Power for non-compliance & as the sole guide of Interpersonal relations, thus replacing the Church. This Research work is important as it will highlight the Evolution of Secularism from medieval times till the Contemporary age in Europe and how the Supremacy of Constitution has substituted the Supremacy of Church thus accommodating different religions, the study will also throw light on the Historical differences between various European States when it came to legitimising the Church. When we compare **Article 4 of the Danish Constitution of 1953** which obliges the State to support the Evangelical-Lutheran Church & addresses it as the "Established Church of Denmark"[1] to **Art.1 of the 1958 Constitution to the French Republic** which states that France shall be a Secular Republic without distinction of any Religion[2] (*laicité*) which implies strict neutrality of the Nation & further goes on to say that the Republic shall not send remuneration in furtherance of a particular Religion & recognizes it in the **Act on the Separation of the State and the Churches of December 1905** goes on to show thestark differences that existed between different European States during the time. This study becomes important in Modern Times as the European Political scenario has increasingly turned to Church Approval with many Politicians promising to impose a Judeo-Christian Government once elected that has put religious minorities in a quandary. From shaping the opinion of mass involved in conflicts like the Russia-Ukraine War in Eastern Europe[3] to supporting politicians[4] that favour increased role of Churches in Public sphere, it becomes all but necessary to trace the origin of the relationship through this study. The evolution of Europe from 1555 principle of Germans & Holy Roman Emperor Charles V of *'cuius region, eius religio'* i.e. religion of the ruler in future would dictate the religion of the Ruled till the Modern times begs the question of the process of alienation of Church from the administration. The first evidence of Religious tolerance can be found in the works of Dutch Philosopher Desiderius Erasmus when he advocated for the same after seeing cracks arising between Catholics & Protestants but did not advocate the same for Muslims & Jews. A contrary view was adopted by John Locke in his *Letters Concerning Toleration* where he advocated for protestant unity & respect forprotestants and discarded forbearance towards Catholics. Similarly, the involvement of Church in Modern Times can be seen in many cases like the Council of European Bishops Conferences (CCEE) that has held in its Plenary meeting that *"State is not capable of determining the meaning of Human Life nor of dealing with Questions that concern the phases in individual's birth..."* and say that Church participation will lead to edification of Europe[5]. In Europe,Churches have also been significant sources of employment & education as they carry out canonical missions that prescribe loyalty to religious ethos like **Article 4.2 of the EU Council Directive 2000/78** that empowers Church as employer to treat employees in ways that mightotherwise be considered out of norms and this research will also address the ways used by Churches for endorsement from State.

**1.1. Research Methodology:** This work follows Doctrinal Method of Research where various articles, statutes & legislations of different European countries have been referred to as primary sources & secondary sources include Journals, books, reports, commentaries and quotes from various biblical sources like reports of the meetings of bishops and publications of various churches. The scholarly works of jurists & philosophers like Gerhard Robbers, Davie, Paul Colton etc. has been cited in the article.

**1.2. Limitations of Research:** The research confines itself to Europe & references made to judgements & practices in U.S. as they follow a similar Western Society & due to constraint of time, budget & doctrinal nature survey conducted by other agencies have been cited.

# CHAPTER THREE

# LITERATURE REVIEW

1. *"Separation of church and state in Europe"* by Fleur de Beaufort and Patrick van Schie[6]

describes the contemporary issues around religion and gives the concept of a 'Foreign Religion' as key to the Secularisation of Europe. It focuses on individual identities and avoids One dimensional categorisation on the basis of Religion, it paints the *laïcité* model as a Weberian ideal type (mental construct). The work does not highlight the humanitarian role of Church.

2. *"The Changing Constitutional Framework of Church-State Relations in Europe"* by Rainer

Grote[7] discusses the various legislations from countries like Denmark, Italy, France etc. to show the influence of Church on State by following the conventional approach but this research aims to highlight a New Modern approach along with the former.

3. *"Church-State Relations in Europe: From Legal Models to an Interdisciplinary Approach"*

by Russell Sandberg[8] although comprehensively spells out the inherent difficulties in analysing Church & State relations from the prism of Constitution by following the three models, it fails to interpret the Hybrid Model of Church-State relations which will be covered by the research.

4. *"Freedom of Religion, Religious Employment, and Conflicts of Rights: Europe at a*

*Crossroads*" by María-José Valero-Estarellas[9] reviews cases from courts of Strasbourg and Luxembourg to test principles like denominational neutrality & show a balance between HR's and Religious Employment but does not analyse the framework from the perspective of Legitimacy of Church and interference in State affairs, leeway in terms of economic employment etc.

5. Aston Cantlow PCC v Wallbank[10] held that PCC under English Church was a core pub. Auth. u/s. 6(1) of HR's Act 1998 without ref. to sub-sec. 3 of the act, when there is clear supremacy of the Monarch, such a judgement imposing liability under the Chancel Repairs Act 1932 on the defendants & petition of Church as victim is also flawed.

# CHAPTER FOUR

# BACKGROUND

**3.1. History of Evolution of Church-State Relationship in Europe: 1)** <u>Church of England:</u> As per Peter Cumper during the Reformation era, Church & State were indistinguishable[11] and similar stance is taken by Richard Hooker in the late 16th C.E. and as per Sir Ernest Barker, nationhood began at Christianity. The Reformation Legislation of 1530s contributed a series of legislations that established Church of England by Law and the expression was used in the canons of law in 1603 as laid down in Canon A7 which states that Monarch is the supreme governor. The Church of England Assembly (Powers) Act, 1919 also known as enabling act empowered the church assembly to repeal/amend existing acts of parliament[12]. 2) <u>Church of Scotland:</u> also known as 'Kirk' was established by the Presbyterian Church Act 1706 later converted into the Church of Scotland Act 1921 which empowered the Church to legislate on all matters concerning doctrine, worship/faith & church governance. The Church Patronage (Scotland) Act 1711 empowered landowners to appoint a parish minister in case of vacancy.

Article 6 of the Danish Constitution of 1953 declares that the Head of the State King shall be a member of the Evangelical Lutheran Church of Denmark and Constitution of the church shall be regulated by parliamentary legislations as per Article 66. Art. 4 of the Swedish Act of Succession also lays down similar provision for the king by mandating that he should follow pure Evangelical Faith as adopted & explained in the Resolution of Uppsala meeting of 1593 and any member disobeying this shall be excluded from Succession. Similarly, Art.4 of the Norwegian Constitution of 1814 states that the King shall follow Evangelical-Lutheran Religion at all times. Art.3 of the Greek Constitution of 1975 refers to the Eastern Orthodox Church as the Prevailing Religion in Greece with over 90% baptized orthodox Christians[13]. The Italian Constitution of 1947 in

Art.7 recognizes the Sovereignty of Catholic church and it also recognized the Authority of Holy See over Vatican City in the Conciliation Treaty[14] & the Concordat between Italian State and Catholic church provided missionary education in schools. In Austria Art.5 of the Concordat guarantees the presence of Catholicism in the Universities of Vienna, Innsbruck & Salzburg. In the case of Forbes v. Eden and others[15] it was held that taking Cognizance of Voluntary organisations like the Church was outside the jurisdiction of courts. In the instant case, the appellant, a member of the Scotch Episcopal Congregation at Burntisland raised an action against the Primus, bishops, deans & other Ministers with summons asking for reduction of some parts of "Code of Canons of Episcopal Church in Scotland". In Aston Cantlow case, Lord Hope of Craighead held that the relationship of Church with the State is not of devolution of Powers.

**3.2. Constitutional Regulations to the State-Church relationship:** Constitutional reforms addressing the relationship between state and Church have been lackadaisical. In England the provision of discontinuing the disqualification of any person marrying a Roman Catholic to the throne was done by the Succession to the Crown Act, 2013. The Constitutional Reform of 2012 removed the provision of Evangelical Lutheran Church as the Official State Religion & replaced it by a general commitment to Norway's Christian Heritage[16] (Grl. § 2) thus laying an example of Separation of Church from State in Modern Europe. The Constitutional Reform went further in § 16 to provide state support to all religious beliefs & the requirement that half of the members of the Norwegian Government must be professing Evangelicalism was also discontinued by § 12 of the act. Similarly, in Italy after 17 years of negotiation, a new concordat was adopted in 1984 that ended the status of Roman Catholic Church as the established Religion & it also took away the powers of church in matters of Religious Education & exemption granted to priests from Civil Law Jurisdiction. These examples show that European Society post reformist movements was heading towards a strict Separation between the Church and the State. There were also Hybrid Systems like Ireland coexisting at the same time where its Constitution provided that "[t]he State guarantees not to endow any religion" & "shall not impose any disabilities or make any discrimination on the ground of religious profession, belief or status"[17] but Article 44(1) in the same spirit states that "[t]he State acknowledges that the homage of public worship is due to Almighty God. It shall hold His Name in reverence, and shall respect and honour religion.". Colton describes the Irish Educational System as a model of Church-State synergy both historically & administratively characterized by "inextricable interdependence"[18]. While in the case of Germany, Monsma & Soper observe that Church-State relations are Characterized by autonomy & cooperation while Robbers adds parity to it.

In France, the causes of Separation between Church & the state have been attributed to appointments made in the clergy by ministers of Worship who promoted agnostics to the position & the miserly stipend of $8mn. p.a. begrudgingly carried with it to certain extent an element of Governmental Supervision thus challenging the independence of the Church[19] which led to the act of 1905. Militant clericals, like M. de Mun, opposed the law by saying that "This law, which assumes the lying name of a separation law, is more odious than the civil constitution of 1791, which, however, left in history a trail of blood. That was a schism; this spells apostasy . . . I hear people say that we must advise Catholics to make a loyal trial of this mortal experiment. As for myself, I shall not consent to it."[20]. Doe recognizes the conventions concerning cooperation b/w. states & religious organizations as informal 'quasi-concordats', a characteristic attributed to hybrid states[21].

**3.2.1. The New Approach to Church-State Relations:** The fact the areas like direction/content of law & religious scholarship gave rise to this interpretation. European Lawyers compiled all laws concerning religion under the broad head of 'ecclesiastical law' which creates differences between commentators & jurists as to its interpretation, for ex: May describes the term as "entirety of the norms of the law laid down by God and by the Church" and excludes all laws regulating church affairs mandated by the state[22]. Huizing draws comparison b/w. Internal & External ecclesiastical law and labelled the former as the Juridical relation within the Church while the Later is the relationship b/w. Church & State[23]. Other works like those of Bradney & Edge adopt relationship thesis which states that the study of religious & legal affairs is the study of their relationship while some more jurists like Malcolm D. Evans & Hamilton follow what may be termed as 'religious freedom thesis' acc. to which this study concerns with religious liberty, a concept inherently embedded with Human Rights study of Church-State relationship as per ECHR. The Sociological work of Grace Davie put the whole continent of Europe on one Religious Pedestal as he argued that the status, role & significance of Religion are common across the Continent as he said that "pattern of unchurched & residual nature of Christianity" is widespread if not Universal across Western Europe[24]

## 3.3. The Different Contours of Church-State Relations & Factors playing role in it:

Religion as a basic freedom overshadowed the traditional framework of State-Church relations. European Convention of Human Rights in Art.9 discusses this aspect[25] & the same is discussed in Art.10 of the Charter on Fundamental Rights of the European Union. It also provides for non-interference in Church & State relations under Art.17 of the Treaty on the Functioning of the European Union[26]. The Grand Chamber in Refah Partisi v. Turkey[27] noted that state's impartial role in promotion of religious tolerance & equality of faith was a "duty" that was imperative in restoring "public order, religious harmony & tolerance in democratic society". Religion as a 'filtering device' can best be seen in the American case of United States v. Kuch[28] where the claimant's claim was that as per her constitutional rights, she could take marijuana and LSD drugs for religious purposes in the Neo-American Church, the Court held that the state had failed in establishing the said body as a church & that it was more for her desire to take it.

The *Reichskonkordat* of 1933 calls the Church-State relationship as sui generis at par with International Treaties. Similarly, in terms of Human Rights, Art.151 of the treaty establishing European Community describes the "idea of a Union that promotes cultural diversity". This spirit is reflected in the case of Kokkinakis v. Greece[29] Where the court reiterated that "Freedom of thought, conscience and religion is one of the foundations of a "democratic society" . . . It is, in its religious dimension, one of the most vital elements that go to make up the identity of believers and their conception of life, but it is also a precious asset to atheists, agnostics, sceptics and the unconcerned. The pluralism indissociable from a democratic society, which has been dearly won over the centuries, depends on it". Despite attempts by figures like Pope Boniface VIII[30] for a Church-State Unity with Papal Supremacy, the reality is far from a Medieval Europe entangled in the Web of Religion, Sanction & Prosecution. Churches also played a role in European integration although scholars like Francois Foret say that EU commission proposes only a limited role for the churches and this results in scarce information on the role of churches on European policies despite their Supranational presence.

# CHAPTER FIVE

# AUTHOR'S ANALYSIS AND CONCLUSION

After observing the theories of various scholars on Church-State Relations in Europe, it can be inferred that the Role of Church in Personal & Constitutional Matters is diminishing & on a downward decline. Although the Church still continues to play a major role in providing healthcare, education (*missio canonica*) & employment. Also, the autonomous space occupied by religious communities is indispensable for a pluralistic society & is protected by Art.9 of ECHR as stated in the case of Fernández Martínez v. Spain[31] which also held that believers of a religion should be given autonomy of associating freely without state intervention. The role of the courts assumes greater importance in overseeing the autonomy enjoyed by the churches by limiting the scope of positive action. The concept of State Church neutrality means that the member states are bound to observe in their interaction with Churches and exercise of State Powers[32]. The court can exercise checks and balances on this relationship like the case of Rommelfanger v. Germany[33] where the commission held that it is the duty of domestic courts to ensure that Churches do not unreasonably enforce their rules. The secularisation of Europe can also be seen from the failure in adoption of Religiously ordained amendments by MEPs like Elmar Brok representing European People's Party & the idea was conceptualized by Adenauer, Monet, De Gasperi and Spaak to the Convention & arguments given for Churchification of Europe were that: Firstly, Population of Europe is overwhelmingly Christian and Secondly, Christian Morals instil in the society an idea of compassion, human dignity & equality of all and lastly it was argued that European Society was influenced by Christian culture preached by saints like St. Augustin in England, St. Bonifacius in Germany, Saints Cyril and Methodius for the Slavic peoples, by reformers such as

Luther or Calvin, by Christian musicians such as Beethoven and Christian artists such as Michaelangelo etc[34]. From this we can conclude that even if Church had interfered in the past with legislations governing the Governor in contemporary times this relationship seems to fade with emerging institutions and a host of various religious beliefs thus confining its role to only Humanitarian assistance.